VICTIMS OF CRIME

GARLAND REFERENCE LIBRARY
OF SOCIAL SCIENCE
(VOL. 139)

VICTIMS OF CRIME
A Research Report of
Experiencing Victimization

Conducted for
Crime Victims Compensation Board,
State of New York

by
Louis Harris and Associates, Inc.
Project Director: Michael J. Bucuvalas

GARLAND PUBLISHING, INC. • NEW YORK & LONDON
1984

Library of Congress Cataloging in Publication Data
Main entry under title:

Victims of crime : a research report of experiencing
  victimization.

  (Garland reference library of social science : v. 139)
  1. Victims of crimes—New York (State) 2. Victims
of crimes—Services for—New York (State) 3. Victims
of crimes surveys—New York (State) I. Louis Harris
and Associates. II. Series.
HV6250.3.U5V53 1984   362.8'8'09747   82-49186
ISBN 0-8240-9145-0 (alk. paper)

Printed on acid-free, 250-year-life paper
Manufactured in the United States of America

ACKNOWLEDGMENT

The publishers gratefully acknowledge the cooperation of the New York State Crime Victims Board which originally commissioned the survey from Louis Harris and Associates, Inc., for the purpose of assessing the service needs, problems and opinions of crime victims in New York State.

TABLE OF CONTENTS

Page

EXECUTIVE SUMMARY.. 1

CHAPTER I: INTRODUCTION... 6

                Objectives of the Survey............................... 6
                Procedures... 7

CHAPTER II: THE CRIME VICTIM AND THE CRIMINAL JUSTICE SYSTEM........... 13

                General Evaluations of How the Police and District Attorney
                    Handled the Case................................... 13
                Specifics of the Criminal Justice System Experience.... 17

CHAPTER III: THE IMPACT OF VICTIMIZATION............................... 21

                Economic Costs... 21
                The Seriousness of Problems Resulting from Victimization.... 27

CHAPTER IV: SERVICES TO CRIME VICTIMS................................. 32

CHAPTER V: THE CRIME VICTIMS COMPENSATION BOARD...................... 36

                Awareness and Contacts................................. 36
                Attitudes of Victims toward the Crime Victims Compensation
                    Board.. 43

INDEX OF TABLES

Table   Page

CHAPTER I: INTRODUCTION

1   TYPE OF CRIME.. 11

2   CHARACTERISTICS OF VICTIMS OF REPORTED CRIMES BY TYPE OF CRIME... 12

CHAPTER II: THE CRIME VICTIM AND THE CRIMINAL JUSTICE SYSTEM

3   SATISFACTION WITH POLICE HANDLING OF CASE BY VWAP CONTACT........ 15

4   SATISFACTION WITH DISTRICT ATTORNEY'S OFFICE BY VWAP CONTACT..... 16

5   ASSESSMENTS OF THE CRIMINAL JUSTICE SYSTEM EXPERIENCE............ 20

CHAPTER III: THE IMPACT OF VICTIMIZATION

6   ECONOMIC IMPACTS OF VICTIMIZATION BY TYPE OF CRIME.............. 24

7   AVERAGE ECONOMIC COSTS (IN HUNDREDS OF DOLLARS) TO VICTIMS
      INCURRING EACH LOSS BY TYPE OF CRIME............................. 25

8   AVERAGE PROPORTION OF COSTS RECOVERED THROUGH INSURANCE.......... 26

9   SERIOUSNESS OF SOCIAL/PSYCHOLOGICAL IMPACTS OF VICTIMIZATION..... 30

10   IMPACT OF CRIME ON VICTIM'S LIFESTYLE BY VWAP CONTACT............ 31

CHAPTER IV: SERVICES TO CRIME VICTIMS

11   VICTIM/WITNESS ASSISTANCE PROGRAM SERVICES RECEIVED.............. 34

12   IMPORTANCE OF VICTIM/WITNESS ASSISTANCE PROGRAMS................. 35

CHAPTER V: THE CRIME VICTIMS COMPENSATION BOARD

13   AWARENESS OF CRIME VICTIMS COMPENSATION BOARD................... 39

(CONTINUED)

INDEX OF TABLES (CONTINUED)

Table		Page
14	HOW LEARNED OF CRIME VICTIMS COMPENSATION BOARD..................	40
15	FILED CLAIM WITH CRIME VICTIMS COMPENSATION BOARD...............	41
16	REASONS FOR NOT FILING A CLAIM WITH CRIME VICTIMS COMPENSATION BOARD..	42
17	APPROVAL OF CRIME VICTIMS COMPENSATION BOARD....................	45
18	SUPPORT FOR INCREASED EXPENDITURES BY CRIME VICTIMS COMPENSATION BOARD..	46
19	SUPPORT FOR PROPOSED CHANGES IN SERVICES TO CRIME VICTIMS........	47

EXECUTIVE SUMMARY

Between December 3, 1980, and February 5, 1981, Louis Harris and Associates interviewed a sample of 450 crime victims who had reported serious crimes to police departments in New York during January and July of 1980. The objective of the survey was to provide initial information on the types of problems faced by crime victims and the usefulness of various types of services to victims in coping with their problems. The results of this pilot survey indicate some of the critical agenda items for dealing with the effects of crime on its victims, but the findings are necessarily limited to the effects on victims of reported crime, since the sample was drawn from the records of police departments in the state.

Victimization affects many different areas of a person's life. Net economic losses averaging over $1,400 per victim and the mental and emotional suffering caused many victims by their experience are only the most obvious consequences. The more subtle effects of the experience may, in fact, be more important by changing how victims feel about themselves, their environment, and the law enforcement system meant to protect them.

More than 3 in 4 victims (78%) of index crimes report having money or property stolen; among these victims, the average loss reported was over $1,500. Somewhat greater costs were incurred for medical expenses by those who required medical treatment ($1,670), but less than 1 in 6 victims (15%) required medical treatment. Some victims recovered their economic losses through insurance and restoration. However, even when these sums are taken into account, the average net loss to victims of reported index crimes in New York State is in excess of $1,400 per victim.

Noneconomic losses, too, have important effects. More than 2 out of 5 victims (43%) rate mental or emotional suffering as a serious problem resulting from their experience. But even more subtle effects occur impacting on victims' lifestyles. More than half (53%) of victims of reported crimes agree with the statement that "being the victim of a crime changed my whole life and made me more fearful about becoming a victim," and 4 out of 5 (82%) agree that "since the crime, I am much more careful about what I do and where I go." Fear is greater among the elderly, minorities, and the poor. These groups also show distinctly higher levels of concern about the <u>dangers</u> involved in testifying against a criminal. The elderly are of particular note in this regard because they are greatly affected psychologically by the crime experience despite having lower incidence of victimization, especially for violent crimes.

Assistance programs for crime victims (VWAP's) can have a major impact in all these areas. They not only alleviate some of the more direct impacts of victimization; the data in this survey indicate that those who received such services were less affected by many of the indirect consequences of victimization as well. Much of the indirect impact of being a victim appears to depend on how victims are treated, and having services available to help them cope with the experience and its consequences is an important element of this. Crime victims themselves indicate that they feel it is important to have these services available, even if they may not have needed them. VWAP services may, thus, have an impact beyond the actual people whom they help directly by creating a climate in which victims have a sense that there are people to help them if they need it.

Almost 1 in 3 victims of reported crime (31%) have received services of the kind offered by Victim/Witness Assistance Programs (VWAP's) from a public agency after the crime occurred. Not all of these victims received services from official VWAP's, but the importance of VWAP-type services for victims is clearly indicated by the survey data.

Those who have received such services rate the criminal justice system more positively than do those who have not. Thus, 73% of those who have had contact with VWAP-type programs are satisfied with how the police handled their case, compared to a lesser 52% of those who have not. And among the 11% of victims who know that arrests were made in their cases, 62% of those who have received VWAP services are satisfied with how the district attorney's office handled their case, compared to 49% of those who have had no VWAP contact.

Although 31% of victims have received some VWAP-type service, very few received any one of the fourteen specific services listed. The most commonly received service was information on case status, received by 10% of victims (20% of those who had arrests made in their cases). However, at least half rate each of the fourteen services as "very important" services to have agencies make available to crime victims. The two highest rated services are compensation for medical expenses and legal assistance (80% and 78% "very important," respectively). The survey data also suggest that there is a shortfall in the availability of VWAP services, as evidenced by the relatively small numbers of victims who received services compared to those who suffered serious problems as a result of victimization.

Turning specifically to the Crime Victims Compensation Board, the survey indicates strong support among victims for the Board's mission. More than 9 out of 10 (93%) crime victims approve of the services provided to victims by the CVCB when these services are explained to them, and 71% would favor providing more money to the Board, even if it meant a slight increase in taxes. Majorities favor each of nine proposals for making changes in the services provided to crime victims in New York State. The strongest support is evidenced for proposals that would recover compensation for victims from criminals.

Although only 2% of all victims of reported crimes have filed claims with the Crime Victims Compensation Board, the percentage of victims who would be eligible for compensation is certainly less than the 15% who reported receiving medical treatment. Thus, the Board is serving a far higher proportion of eligible victims than indicated by the 2% figure. Nevertheless, only 35% of all victims had ever heard of the CVCB before this survey. Of these (including those who were injured), very few had learned about CVCB from police; the most common way to have learned about the Board was from the media (television and radio spot announcements and newspapers). The primary reasons given by the 1 in 3 victims who knew of the Board but did not file a claim are that the claim was too small (38%) or that they did not expect to qualify (30%).

Thus, this pilot survey indicates a number of clear directions. First, there is certainly room for expanding the VWAP services available to victims. In particular, services that lessen the trauma of the victimization experience and that humanize the treatment of victims may be of great importance. VWAP services appear to be especially critical for the elderly and minority groups in this regard -- reducing some of the special psychological impact of victimization on these groups. Second, further effort is needed in communicating the availability of services to victims. This is most clearly notable in police notification of victims about the services offered by the CVCB; the data indicate that this legislatively mandated procedure is only rarely being followed. Finally, there is a need to follow up this pilot study with research that probes specific issues in greater detail. The need for further research is most pressing for those groups -- especially, the elderly and minorities -- which are particularly affected by the victimization experience; further study and larger samples would allow more detailed specification of the problems these groups face and of what can be done to help them. This survey takes the first steps in indicating the critical directions to be taken in the planning and analysis of efforts to assist crime victims and the basic importance of pursuing such efforts.

CHAPTER I: INTRODUCTION

Between December 3, 1980, and February 5, 1981, Louis Harris and Associates interviewed a sample of 450 victims of serious crimes who had reported these crimes to police departments in the state of New York during either January or July of 1980. This pilot survey -- sponsored by the New York State Crime Victims Compensation Board -- indicates a number of critical agenda items for dealing with the effects of crime on its victims.

Until recently, public policy toward crime has focused on the criminal and ignored the victim. When the Crime Victims Compensation Board was established in 1966, it was one of the first public agencies in the field. The Board, however, has not been a general purpose victim assistance agency. Its legislative mandate is to alleviate the financial hardships of crime for innocent victims (and their dependents) who are injured, disabled, or killed as a result of violent crimes. More recently, a wider array of services, assistance, and types of compensation have been offered by other agencies under the generic heading of Victim/Witness Assistance Programs (VWAP's). Such programs have been established in both the State of New York and other states.

Objectives of the Survey

The objectives of this pilot survey of the victims of reported crime are to establish both the methodological and substantive bases for a fuller assessment of the needs of crime victims and the role of public policy in meeting these needs. Specifically, the substantive issues to be addressed are:

- The cost of victimization, including the social and psychological as well as the economic costs;

- The experience of victims with the criminal justice system;

- The services received by victims from VWAP-type programs;

- The effect of receiving VWAP-type services on victims and their assessment of the criminal justice system;

- Victims' familiarity and evaluation of the Crime Victims Compensation Board; and

- Proposed changes in the services offered to crime victims in New York State.

Procedures

The sample of 450 crime victims interviewed in this survey was selected by a two-stage process: first, police departments were chosen, and second, individuals were selected from among those reporting crimes to each department in either January or July of 1980.

Only victims reporting index crimes (not including auto theft) were included in the universe from which the sample was drawn; in the tabular presentations in this report, the 2 respondents interviewed as family members of murder victims are excluded because their experiences are qualitatively different from those of other victims. Thus, the sample size for the quantitative analysis in this report is 448. Police departments were chosen in the first step by a procedure that made the likelihood of their selection dependent on the number of index crimes (not including auto theft) reported in their jurisdictions. Departments outside of the New York City metropolitan area were slightly oversampled, and in the analysis below the data have been weighted to reflect the appropriate incidence by type of community and area of the state. For each department selected, 10 interviews were conducted with victims selected randomly from those reporting index crimes other than auto theft in either January, 1980 (5 interviews), or July, 1980 (5 interviews). This procedure yields a sample that is representative of reported crime victimization statewide, with the caveats indicated below.

All interviews for this survey were conducted by telephone from the Harris interviewing facility in New York City. The level of cooperation with the survey was very high, with 12% of victims who were contacted not completing the interview. However, a large proportion (46%) of the telephone numbers provided the Harris firm by the Board staff (secured either from police department records or New York Telephone listings) proved to be unusable; the major problems were that the telephone number was incorrect (15%), that the listed individual was not a victim (12%), that the number was no longer in service (9%), or that the victim died or moved away (6%).

The focus on reported crime and the followup of these reports by telephone place certain constraints on the ability to generalize from the sample results. The primary effect is to underrepresent poorer crime victims and the impact of victimization on the poor. A number of different elements of the survey design all work in this same direction.

First, it is generally accepted that poorer victims are less likely to report crimes. Therefore, a sample based on reported crimes will underrepresent poor victims. On the other hand, public services to crime victims are meant to coordinate with the criminal justice system and are likely to be available only to victims who report the crimes committed against them. Thus, a sample based on reported crimes has more relevance to the issues addressed by this survey. Nevertheless, it must be recalled in reading the findings of this study that the results apply only to the victims of reported index crimes.

Second, as outlined above, not all victims listed in police records were reached. The effects of disconnected or unlisted numbers, of incorrect numbers, and of victims having moved may all be considered to have occurred disproportionately among poorer victims.

The design of the sampling procedure explicitly aims to correct some of the undersampling of poorer victims. For each police department (or precinct within New York City) in the sample, at least 10 interviews were completed with victims from the department's lists. This procedure guaranteed that appropriate numbers of victims from lower income areas were included in the sample.

Finally, where differences in the responses of victims in different income groups are notable, we have reported these differences in either the tables or the text. In such cases, the true figure for the total victim population of New York State will be closer to the percentage shown for low income groups than to the figure shown for the total sample, to the extent that poorer victims are, in fact, underrepresented. On the whole, the differences between income groups are relatively modest, suggesting that any underrepresentation of poorer victims may not have great effects when the universe is limited to victims of reported crimes.

However, the limitation that only victims of reported crime are included in the sample should not be neglected. Further, this is a pilot survey, with a limited sample. For a question where answers are split 50-50%, the sampling error is ±5 percentage points; that is, 19 times out of 20, we would expect the figures from a sample of this size (448) to fall within +5 percentage points of the results that would be obtained by interviewing all victims of reported crime in New York State. For subgroups of the total population margins for sampling error are larger.

Table 1 presents a breakdown of respondents by the type of crime reported and Table 2 a brief demographic profile of the sample. These descriptive data serve as background to some of the analyses to follow. It should be noted that percentages in tables may not always sum to exactly 100% because of rounding or the acceptance of multiple responses.

Q.1A

TABLE 1

TYPE OF CRIME

Q.: Police department records show that you reported that either you or a member of your family were the victim of a crime in the past twelve months. How would you describe that crime you reported -- was it a mugging, a robbery, an assault, a burglary, a rape, a murder, or what? (IF VICTIM MORE THAN ONCE: ASK ABOUT MOST RECENT TIME)

	TOTAL
BASE	447
	%
MUGGING	12
ROBBERY	30
ASSAULT	14
BURGLARY	39
RAPE	2
LARCENY	2
ATTEMPTED RAPE	2
MURDER	*
OTHER	*

*LESS THAN 0.5%.

BANNER X BANNER

TABLE 2

CHARACTERISTICS OF VICTIMS OF REPORTED CRIMES
BY TYPE OF CRIME

		TYPE OF CRIME				
BASE	TOTAL	MUGGING	ROBBERY	ASSAULT	BURGLARY	OTHER
	448	54	135	61	176	33
	%	%	%	%	%	%
COUNTY TYPE						
URBAN	75	9.8	74	65	72	76
SUBURBAN	20	2	19	25	24	19
RURAL	5	-	7	10	4	5
REGION						
METRO NEW YORK	70	84	69	80	62	74
UPSTATE	30	16	31	20	38	26
RACE						
WHITE	67	47	65	61	75	75
BLACK	21	34	25	26	15	15
HISPANIC	9	19	6	12	7	6
INCOME						
$15,000 OR LESS	42	53	37	49	41	45
$15,001-$35,000	36	24	42	33	37	28
$35,001 AND OVER	10	2	11	8	13	9
AGE						
UNDER 30 YEARS	30	25	35	47	20	48
30-64 YEARS	61	60	57	53	67	48
65 AND OVER	9	15	8	-	13	3

CHAPTER II: THE CRIME VICTIM AND THE CRIMINAL JUSTICE SYSTEM

Only 11% of victims who reported index crimes are aware that arrests were made in their cases, and only about 1 in 5 of these (22%) are aware that the suspects have been brought to trial and found guilty. Overall, therefore, only 2% of those victims who have reported crimes can be said to have observed a complete resolution of their cases. This is the context in which these victims assess their experience with the criminal justice system.

General Evaluations of How the Police and District Attorney Handled the Case

Victims of reported index crimes in New York State give the police a positive rating on handling their case. Overall, almost 3 out of 5 (59%) are satisfied with how the case was handled; one-third (33%) are very satisfied (Table 3). Blacks are more likely than whites to be dissatisfied with how the police handled the case (45% vs. 31%), and rural residents are more dissatisfied than urban residents (54% vs. 32%). On the other hand, elderly victims (65 years and older) are the group most likely to be very satisfied with the police (47% compared with 33% of the sample as a whole).

A critical difference is observed between those who received services of the type offered by Victim/Witness Assistance Programs and those who did not. Almost 3 out of 4 victims (73%) who received VWAP-type services are satisfied with how the police handled the case, compared with about half (52%) of those who did not receive such services. As Table 3 indicates, most of the difference occurs in the "somewhat satisfied" category; 34% of those who had

VWAP contacts are somewhat satisfied with the way the police handled the case, compared with only 22% of those who did not have VWAP contacts.

The rating of the way the district attorney's office handled the case among those who say that an arrest was made in their case is quite similar to the rating of the police department among the sample as a whole: 57% satisfied vs. 28% dissatisfied (Table 4). Again, the rating among victims who have received VWAP-type services is more positive (62% satisfied) than the rating among those who received no such services (49% satisfied); however, because only 50 victims say that arrests were made in their case, this difference must be treated as mainly suggestive and supportive of the effects of VWAP's observed for ratings of the police.

Observation:

While other factors are operating, the data demonstrate that VWAP services play an important role in improving victims' assessments of criminal justice system agencies. This effect can be traced largely to VWAP services giving victims a greater sense that someone in the system cares about their problems and is willing to do something about them.

The differences in ratings among various social groups can probably be traced to the differing expectations of the groups. For instance, the high level of "very satisfied" ratings of the police among the elderly may be related to the fact that older people have the highest incidence of burglaries of any group in the sample; if they expected only minimal responsiveness from the police for this type of crime and instead received a certain amount of sympathy and possibly some advice on the security of their homes, they might have been very satisfied simply because of their low initial expectations.

Q.5

TABLE 3

SATISFACTION WITH POLICE HANDLING OF CASE BY VWAP CONTACT

Q.: I'd like to know how you felt about the way the police handled your case. Overall, were you very satisfied, somewhat satisfied, somewhat dissatisfied, or very dissatisfied with the way the police handled your case?

		VICTIM/ WITNESS ASSISTANCE PROGRAM CONTACT*	
	TOTAL	YES	NO
BASE	448	137	311
	%	%	%
VERY SATISFIED	33	39	30
SOMEWHAT SATISFIED	26	34	22
SOMEWHAT DISSATISFIED	15	9	18
VERY DISSATISFIED	18	12	20
NOT SURE	8	5	10

*VICTIM/WITNESS ASSISTANCE PROGRAM (VWAP) CONTACTS ARE DEFINED IN TERMS OF RESPONDENTS' HAVING RECEIVED THE TYPES OF SERVICES VWAP'S OFFER AFTER HAVING BEEN VICTIMIZED. SOME SERVICES MAY HAVE BEEN PROVIDED BY PROGRAMS THAT ARE NOT FORMALLY VWAP'S, BUT PROVIDED SIMILAR SERVICES TO THESE VICTIMS. SEE TABLE 11 FOR THE RESPONSES TO Q.10A ABOUT RECEIVING VWAP SERVICES.

Q.7A

TABLE 4

SATISFACTION WITH DISTRICT ATTORNEY'S OFFICE BY VWAP CONTACT
BASE: YES, SOMEONE ARRESTED

Q.: How did you feel about the way the district attorney's office handled your case -- overall, were you very satisfied, somewhat satisfied, somewhat dissatisfied, or very dissatisfied with the way the district attorney's office handled your case?

		VICTIM/ WITNESS ASSISTANCE PROGRAM CONTACT*	
	TOTAL	YES	NO
BASE	50	29	21
	%	%	%
VERY SATISFIED	32	41	20
SOMEWHAT SATISFIED	25	21	29
SOMEWHAT DISSATISFIED	2	4	-
VERY DISSATISFIED	26	24	28
NOT SURE	16	10	23

*VICTIM/WITNESS ASSISTANCE PROGRAM (VWAP) CONTACTS ARE DEFINED IN TERMS OF RESPONDENTS' HAVING RECEIVED THE TYPES OF SERVICES VWAP'S OFFER AFTER HAVING BEEN VICTIMIZED. SOME SERVICES MAY HAVE BEEN PROVIDED BY PROGRAMS THAT ARE NOT FORMALLY VWAP'S, BUT PROVIDED SIMILAR SERVICES TO THESE VICTIMS. SEE TABLE 11 FOR THE RESPONSES TO Q.10A ABOUT RECEIVING VWAP SERVICES.

Specifics of the Criminal Justice System Experience

The overall evaluations of the criminal justice system appear to be more closely linked to <u>how</u> the victims were treated than to what was actually done by the police and the district attorney's office. This is implicit in the high level of satisfaction with criminal justice agencies reported by victims despite the low incidence of arrests and convictions. It is made explicit in victims' responses about specific aspects of their experience with the criminal justice system (Table 5).

Large majorities of these victims of reported crime rate the criminal justice system positively on the way in which they were treated:

-- By 86-11%, victims agree that "the police treated me well";

-- By 76-17%, they disagree with the statement that "during the whole period I was treated more like the criminal than like the victim";

-- By 75-21%, they agree that "the police responded quickly after they were told of the crime."

As a result, an overwhelming majority (83-13%) reject the idea that after this experience with the criminal justice system they "wouldn't ever bother to get involved with the police or the courts again."

On the other hand, fewer than half (45%) agree that "the police did all they could to try to locate the criminal," and 1 in 3 victims (34%) disagree with this statement, with another 18% not sure of whether the police did all they could or not. Thus, in total, 52% of victims express doubt about the effort the police made to apprehend the criminal.

Nor do these victims feel they were kept well informed about what was going on. By an almost 2-to-1 margin (59-30%) they agree that they were "not kept informed about what was happening during the police investigation of the crime"; even among those victims who know that an arrest was made in their case, 51% agree with this statement while only 42% disagree. Similar doubts are expressed about the trial stage of the investigation, with 7% agreeing that they "were not kept informed of what was happening during the trial," and only 6% disagreeing (with 86% saying the statement does not apply to their case).

Thus, although 58% reject the statement that "nobody in the criminal justice system seems to care about the victim," more than one-third of victims (36%) agree with that statement.

The effect of VWAP-type services is clearly demonstrated on this issue. Among those who received VWAP services, 64% reject the idea that nobody cares about the victim, compared with 55% who disagree with the statement among those who did not receive VWAP services. In fact, disagreement with this statement is higher among those who received VWAP services (64%) than it is even among those who report that an arrest was made in their case (51%).

The importance of the way in which victims are treated is further illustrated in the case of black victims. They rate the overall police handling of their case lower than do whites (50% satisfied vs. 60% satisfied). On each of the three treatment items, they are less positive than whites.

-- By 82% to 87%, blacks are less likely to agree that "the police treated me well";

-- By 22% to 15%, blacks are more likely to agree that they were "treated more like the criminal than like the victim";

-- By 66% to 77%, blacks are less likely to feel that "the police responded quickly after they were told of the crime."

Moreover, the two items on serving as a witness indicate that while many people are concerned about their safety if they testify, this concern is highest among minority groups and the elderly. Although more than half of the victims (52%) agree that "identifying a subject or testifying in court is dangerous because they may try to get even with you," only 24% agree that they would not testify "because the punishment [criminals] would get is not worth the risk they will try to get even." Thus, despite their concerns, most victims would be willing to testify. However, strong agreement that there are dangers involved in testifying is markedly higher among minority victims (47%) and among elderly victims (45%) than it is among victims in general (29%). This higher level of concern is reflected in the fact that 23% of minority victims and 30% of elderly victims agree strongly that they "will never take the chance of testifying against someone," compared with only 15% of victims in general.

Observation:

The importance of how victims are treated by the criminal justice system is strongly emphasized in these data. Victims' satisfaction with the criminal justice system appears to depend more on demonstrating that people care about their experience than on the direct resolution of their case. VWAP services embody the public concern for victims' problems and raise victims' satisfaction with the criminal justice system.

Q.8

TABLE 5

ASSESSMENTS OF THE CRIMINAL JUSTICE SYSTEM EXPERIENCE

Q.: Now I'd like to read a series of statements about being the victim of a crime. Some crime victims agree with these statements; other crime victims disagree with these statements. On the basis of your experience, please tell me whether you agree strongly, agree somewhat, disagree somewhat, or disagree strongly with each statement?

BASE: 447	AGREE STRONGLY %	AGREE SOMEWHAT %	DISAGREE SOMEWHAT %	DISAGREE STRONGLY %	NO EXPERIENCE/ DOES NOT APPLY (VOL.) %	NOT SURE %
THE POLICE TREATED ME WELL	68	18	4	7	1	2
THE POLICE RESPONDED QUICKLY AFTER THEY WERE TOLD OF THE CRIME	61	14	6	15	1	3
I WAS NOT KEPT INFORMED ABOUT WHAT WAS HAPPENING DURING THE POLICE INVESTIGATION OF THE CRIME	43	16	10	20	9	3
THE POLICE DID ALL THEY COULD TO TRY TO LOCATE THE CRIMINAL	31	14	13	21	3	18
IDENTIFYING A SUBJECT OR TESTIFYING IN COURT IS DANGEROUS BECAUSE THEY MAY TRY TO GET EVEN WITH YOU	29	23	16	23	5	4
THE WHOLE EXPERIENCE OF THE INVESTIGATION AND TRIAL WAS VERY DISTURBING TO ME	22	10	13	24	28	3
NOBODY IN THE CRIMINAL JUSTICE SYSTEM SEEMS TO CARE ABOUT THE VICTIM	21	15	27	31	*	5
I WILL NEVER TAKE THE CHANCE OF TESTIFYING AGAINST SOMEONE BECAUSE THE PUNISHMENT THEY WOULD GET IS NOT WORTH THE RISK THEY WILL TRY TO GET EVEN	15	9	21	44	7	5
DURING THE WHOLE PERIOD I WAS TREATED MORE LIKE THE CRIMINAL THAN LIKE THE VICTIM	12	5	16	60	4	4
AFTER MY EXPERIENCE IN THIS CASE, I WOULDN'T EVER BOTHER TO GET INVOLVED WITH THE POLICE OR THE COURTS AGAIN	9	4	17	66	1	3
I WAS NOT KEPT INFORMED OF WHAT WAS HAPPENING DURING THE TRIAL	5	2	1	5	86	2

*LESS THAN 0.5%.

CHAPTER III: THE IMPACT OF VICTIMIZATION

Crime impacts on its victims in a number of ways. The most obvious way is the economic cost directly associated with the crime -- e.g., property stolen by a burglar. There are also less direct economic costs, such as the medical treatment for injuries resulting from the incident and loss of time from work either because of injury or because of working with the criminal justice system. In addition to the economic costs, there are also psychological and social costs imposed on the victim. The fact that it is hard to place a dollar value on these costs does not make them any less real for the victims themselves. In this chapter, we will examine these various costs sustained by victims of reported crime in New York State.

Economic Costs

The first step in assessing economic costs is to determine how many victims incur various forms of economic loss. The most frequently incurred cost for victims of reported crime is having money or property stolen (Table 6). While over three-quarters of victims (78%) report having money or property stolen, fewer than half say they incurred each of the other costs listed.

However, while only 15% of the crime victims report that they received medical treatment or spent time in the hospital, medical costs tended to be the most expensive of the economic costs when they were incurred (Table 7). Thus, the average cost of medical treatment resulting from injuries related to the crime was $1,670 for those who received medical treatment for their injuries. In addition, an average of $800 was lost by those who missed time from work because of their injuries. The next most expensive impact was the $1,550 average loss for money or property stolen. The value of property damaged or destroyed was considerably less (averaging $440).

Finally, although the costs of time lost from work to help the police (averaging $130) or the district attorney's office (averaging $150) were the least expensive economic costs, these costs were not minor. Further, these costs were also incurred by those victims who say that an arrest was not made in their case. In fact, the average dollar value of time lost from work to assist the district attorney's office was higher among those reporting that no arrest was made ($170) than among those reporting an arrest ($140). However, the cost of time lost from work to help the police in the investigation was higher among those victims reporting that an arrest was made in their case ($210) than among those not reporting an arrest ($110).

However, because the incidence of money or property being stolen is much higher than the incidence of other economic losses as a result of crime victimization, the overall economic cost resulting from money or property being stolen is higher than the overall economic cost resulting from each of the other types of losses. For instance, when the economic costs are averaged over all victims of reported index crimes, the average value of money or property stolen per victim ($1,209) is almost five times larger than the average cost of medical treatment ($250).

Most of the costs incurred by victims of crime were not reimbursed to them (Table 8). The best levels of reimbursement are reported for medical expenses, but only one-third of these expenses were reimbursed for the average victim. Of greater economic impact is the fact that only 15.9% of losses for stolen money or property were reimbursed on average, leaving the average crime victim with a net loss of over $1,000 in stolen money or property.

Observation:

Being victimized can be expensive. The average victim incurs a net loss of over $1,000 dollars in stolen money or property, approximately $170 in medical expenses, and almost $150 in property that is damaged or destroyed, as well as the additional cost of time lost from work that can bring the total net cost to the average victim of a reported index crime in New York State to over $1,400.

Q.9A

TABLE 6

ECONOMIC IMPACTS OF VICTIMIZATION BY TYPE OF CRIME

Q.: I'm going to read you a list of things that might have happened to you as a result of being a crime victim. Please tell me which ones actually happened to you. To start with, did you (READ EACH ITEM) or not?

		TYPE OF CRIME				
BASE	TOTAL	MUGGING	ROBBERY	ASSAULT	BURGLARY	OTHER
	448	54	135	61	176	33
	%	%	%	%	%	%
HAVE MONEY OR PROPERTY STOLEN						
YES	78	85	96	24	91	37
NO	22	15	4	76	9	63
NOT SURE	–	–	–	–	–	–
HAVE PROPERTY DAMAGED OR DESTROYED		.				
YES	40	11	41	34	55	38
NO	59	89	58	66	45	62
NOT SURE	*	–	1	–	–	–
LOSE TIME FROM WORK TO PROVIDE INFORMATION TO POLICE FOR THE INVESTIGATION						
YES	19	13	22	26	18	14
NO	81	87	78	74	82	86
NOT SURE	–	–	–	–	–	–
PERSONALLY RECEIVE ANY PHYSICAL INJURIES AS A RESULT OF THE CRIME						
YES	19	40	9	74	1	24
NO	81	60	91	26	99	76
NOT SURE	–	–	–	–	–	–
RECEIVE MEDICAL TREATMENT OR SPEND TIME IN THE HOSPITAL AS A RESULT OF INJURIES						
YES	15	24	5	60	1	26
NO	85	76	94	40	99	74
NOT SURE	*	–	1	–	–	–
LOSE TIME FROM WORK BECAUSE OF INJURIES						
YES	9	15	2	35	4	9
NO	91	85	98	65	96	91
NOT SURE	–	–	–	–	–	–
LOSE TIME FROM WORK TO ASSIST THE DISTRICT ATTORNEY OR TAKE PART IN THE TRIAL						
YES	6	2	7	14	4	3
NO	93	98	92	83	95	97
NOT SURE	1	–	1	3	1	–

*LESS THAN 0.5%.

Q.9B

TABLE 7

AVERAGE ECONOMIC COSTS (IN HUNDREDS OF DOLLARS) TO VICTIMS
INCURRING EACH LOSS BY TYPE OF CRIME
BASE: HAD EACH TYPE OF IMPACT

Q.: I would like you to estimate the dollar value of each of these things. For
instance, how much would you estimate it cost you in dollars to (READ EACH ITEM "YES" IN
Q.9a)?

	TOTAL	TYPE OF CRIME				
		MUGGING	ROBBERY	ASSAULT	BURGLARY	OTHER
RECEIVE MEDICAL TREATMENT OR SPEND TIME IN THE HOSPITAL AS A RESULT OF INJURIES	16.7	2.9	6.9	25.0	13.3	.5
HAVE MONEY OR PROPERTY STOLEN	15.5	7.0	12.0	10.8	21.5	14.9
LOSE TIME FROM WORK BECAUSE OF INJURIES	8.0	9.5	.7	10.2	5.7	6.3
HAVE PROPERTY DAMAGED OR DESTROYED	4.4	1.3	6.3	2.4	4.2	2.9
LOSE TIME FROM WORK TO ASSIST THE DISTRICT ATTORNEY OR TAKE PART IN THE TRIAL	1.5	-	1.3	1.9	2.0	.4
LOSE TIME FROM WORK TO PROVIDE INFORMATION TO POLICE FOR THE INVESTIGATION	1.3	.3	1.3	1.7	1.5	.4

Q.9C

TABLE 8

AVERAGE PROPORTION OF COSTS RECOVERED THROUGH INSURANCE
BASE: HAD EACH TYPE OF IMPACT

Q.: What percentage of this cost would you estimate you recovered through insurance or any other means?

	TOTAL
LOSE TIME FROM WORK BECAUSE OF INJURIES	12.7%
LOSE TIME FROM WORK TO PROVIDE INFORMATION TO POLICE FOR THE INVESTIGATION	3.3%
LOSE TIME FROM WORK TO ASSIST THE DISTRICT ATTORNEY OR TAKE PART IN THE TRIAL	9.2%
HAVE MONEY OR PROPERTY STOLEN	15.9%
HAVE PROPERTY DAMAGED OR DESTROYED	16.7%
RECEIVE MEDICAL TREATMENT OR SPEND TIME IN THE HOSPITAL AS A RESULT OF INJURIES	33.0%

The Seriousness of Problems Resulting from Victimization

Not all costs are easily quantifiable, nor is the impact of a particular dollar amount the same for all victims. Therefore, the survey also asked how serious a problem each of eight types of impact were for the victims (Table 9).

Clearly, property loss presents a serious problem to the greatest number of victims. With 78% of all victims averaging $1,550 in losses for stolen money or property and 40% averaging $440 in losses for property damaged or destroyed, the finding that 56% of victims consider property loss a serious problem is to be expected.

The problem next most likely to be rated as serious is mental or emotional suffering; 18% of victims rate this as very serious and another 25% rate it as somewhat serious. Mental or emotional suffering is more likely to be a serious problem for victims of assault (56% very or somewhat serious) or mugging (52%) than for victims of index crimes in general (43%).

Fewer victims feel that the other impacts are serious; in fact, each of the others is seen by more than 3 out of 5 victims to be "not a problem at all."

Observation:

Property losses and mental or emotional suffering are the problems that are most likely to be serious for victims of index crimes. However, this does not mean that the other problems are not very serious to those who face them. We have seen that, for those who experienced them, the dollar losses resulting from injury were greater than those resulting from theft or property losses. Moreover, very few victims may have problems with their jobs resulting from the crime, but the loss of a job for reasons relating

to the crime would be very serious. Therefore, the
likelihood of a problem being serious for victims in
general should not be confused with the impact of a
particular problem on any individual victim.

Victimization also has a more generalized effect. It can make crime

victims rethink their basic attitudes and change their social relationships.

Thus, 4 out of 5 victims (82%) agree that "since the crime, I am more careful

about what I do and where I go" (Table 10). This feeling is strong among all

groups of victims; it is particularly strong among victims of muggings (94%),

but it even extends to burglary victims (81%). The strength of this sentiment

is indicated by the fact that 63% of victims agree strongly with the statement.

A majority of victims (53%) even agree with the much stronger

statement that "being the victim of a crime changed my whole life and made me

more fearful about becoming a victim." Only 44% of victims reject the idea

that the experience changed their whole lives and made them more fearful.

Agreement that the crime changed their whole lives is strongest for certain

population groups: women (70%), minority victims (68%), the elderly (64%),

victims with family incomes below $15,000 (63%), and residents of the New York

City metropolitan area (58%). And while there is agreement with this

sentiment among victims of all types of index crimes, it is strongest among

mugging victims (79%). On the other hand, VWAP-type services again appear to

reduce the impact of victimization; 45% of those who have received VWAP-type

services agree that the crime changed their whole lives, compared with 57% of

those who have not received such services.

Observation:

The subtle effects of victimization on people's lifestyles
and self-confidence may in some ways be the most pervasive
and most serious effects of crime. By making people more
fearful, crime can change the very nature of the social
fabric. The fact that this impact falls more heavily on
some social groups than on others can serve as a serious
disadvantage and impediment to these groups. This is
doubly significant since most of the groups on which the
effect is greatest already are less advantaged. That
VWAP's may alleviate some of this effect is especially
critical, suggesting that by targeting the delivery of
these services some of the special impact on these groups
might be reduced.

Q.11

TABLE 9

SERIOUSNESS OF SOCIAL/PSYCHOLOGICAL IMPACTS OF VICTIMIZATION

Q.: As a result of the incident, (was/were) (READ EACH ITEM) a very serious problem, somewhat serious, not too serious, or not a problem at all?

BASE: 448	VERY SERIOUS %	SOMEWHAT SERIOUS %	NOT TOO SERIOUS %	NOT A PROBLEM AT ALL %	NOT SURE %
PROPERTY LOSS	30	26	18	25	1
MENTAL OR EMOTIONAL SUFFERING	18	25	18	39	*
INCOME LOSS	17	10	11	63	*
INSURANCE PROBLEMS	13	13	10	63	2
TIME LOST FROM YOUR WORK	12	10	10	68	*
PROBLEMS WITH YOUR FAMILY	10	13	7	69	*
PHYSICAL INJURY	8	6	7	79	-
PROBLEMS WITH YOUR JOB	7	7	6	80	*

*LESS THAN 0.5%.

Q.8

TABLE 10

IMPACT OF CRIME ON VICTIM'S LIFESTYLE BY VWAP CONTACT

Q.: Now I'd like to read a series of statements about being the victim of a crime. Some crime victims agree with these statements; other crime victims disagree with these statements. On the basis of your experience, please tell me whether you agree strongly, agree somewhat, disagree somewhat, or disagree strongly with each statement?

		VICTIM/ WITNESS ASSISTANCE PROGRAM CONTACT*	
	TOTAL	YES	NO
BASE	447	137	310
	%	%	%
SINCE THE CRIME, I AM MUCH MORE CAREFUL ABOUT WHAT I DO AND WHERE I GO			
AGREE STRONGLY	63	57	65
AGREE SOMEWHAT	19	22	18
DISAGREE SOMEWHAT	5	8	4
DISAGREE STRONGLY	11	11	11
NO EXPERIENCE/DOES NOT APPLY (VOL.)	2	1	2
NOT SURE	1	1	1
BEING THE VICTIM OF A CRIME CHANGED MY WHOLE LIFE AND MADE ME MORE FEARFUL ABOUT BECOMING A VICTIM			
AGREE STRONGLY	38	29	42
AGREE SOMEWHAT	15	16	15
DISAGREE SOMEWHAT	18	20	16
DISAGREE STRONGLY	26	32	24
NO EXPERIENCE/DOES NOT APPLY (VOL.)	1	2	1
NOT SURE	1	1	2

*VICTIM/WITNESS ASSISTANCE PROGRAM (VWAP) CONTACTS ARE DEFINED IN TERMS OF RESPONDENTS' HAVING RECEIVED THE TYPES OF SERVICES VWAP'S OFFER AFTER HAVING BEEN VICTIMIZED. SOME SERVICES MAY HAVE BEEN PROVIDED BY PROGRAMS THAT ARE NOT FORMALLY VWAP'S, BUT PROVIDED SIMILAR SERVICES TO THESE VICTIMS. SEE TABLE 11 FOR THE RESPONSES TO Q.10A ABOUT RECEIVING VWAP SERVICES.

CHAPTER IV: SERVICES TO CRIME VICTIMS

Almost 1 out of 3 victims (31%) received some service of the kind offered by Victim/Witness Assistance Programs (VWAP's) from a public agency after the crime occurred. Not all of these victims received these services from programs that are officially VWAP's, no doubt, but the effect of these services on victims' attitudes toward their experience has been indicated by a number of findings in this report. In this chapter, we take a brief look at the nature of these services.

The fourteen services asked about in this survey illustrate the diversity of services that may be offered victims. The responses demonstrate that no specific service was received by any large number of victims (Table 11). The most commonly received VWAP-type service was information on case status; 10% of victims received information on their case status from some social service or government agency (20% of those who report that an arrest was made in their case). Security information or assistance was provided to 8% of victims of reported crime, and 6% got their property back or money to replace the property. The other eleven services listed were each received by less than 5% of the victims of reported index crimes in New York State.

Crime victims think that it is important to have agencies that make each and every one of these fourteen services available to victims. Half or more of the victims rate having each of these services available as very important, and the percentages rating having these services available for

victims as either very or somewhat important range from a high of 94% to a
very high low of 79% (Table 12). Compensation for medical expenses and legal
assistance are each rated important by 94% of victims. But even the service
that gets the lowest importance rating -- relocation or help in finding a new
residence -- is rated important by 79%, and only 6% of victims rate it not
important at all.

Observation:

The importance of having VWAP services available does not
mean that each of these victims personally needed these
services or would have used them had they been available.
The data on the seriousness of various problem areas in the
previous chapter indicate that the bulk of these services
were not needed by many of the crime victims. What these
data say clearly is that crime victims are almost unanimous
in feeling that these services should be there for those
who do, in fact, need them. And the data on actual
utilization go further -- to suggest that there is a
serious shortfall in the availability of these services.
From the data on the impact of victimization, it is evident
that many more victims could have benefited from these
services, and other survey data indicate that this would
have contributed greatly to reducing the impact of
victimization on these people's lives and on their
attitudes towards the criminal justice system. VWAP
services are, thus, an area in which there is a clear need
for expanded service availability.

Q.10A

TABLE 11

VICTIM/WITNESS ASSISTANCE PROGRAM SERVICES RECEIVED

Q.: After the crime occurred, did you receive (READ EACH ITEM) from any social service or government agency?

BASE: 448	YES %	NO %	DOES NOT APPLY (VOL.) %	NOT SURE %
INFORMATION ON YOUR CASE STATUS	10	81	8	1
SECURITY INFORMATION OR ASSISTANCE	8	89	3	*
THE PROPERTY BACK OR MONEY TO REPLACE THE PROPERTY	6	85	9	*
LEGAL ASSISTANCE	4	92	4	-
INFORMATION AND REFERRALS FOR SERVICES	4	91	5	*
ASSISTANCE IN DEALING WITH THE POLICE, COURTS, OR SOCIAL SERVICES	4	90	6	-
EMOTIONAL OR PSYCHOLOGICAL COUNSELING	3	92	5	*
COMPENSATION FOR MEDICAL EXPENSES	3	60	37	*
COMPENSATION FOR STOLEN PROPERTY	3	88	9	-
PERSONAL PROTECTION	3	93	4	*
TRANSPORTATION TO THE COURTS	2	56	42	-
COMPENSATION FOR LOSS OF EARNINGS OR SUPPORT	2	77	21	-
RELOCATION OR HELP IN FINDING A NEW RESIDENCE	1	85	14	-
DAY CARE FOR YOUR CHILDREN	*	70	29	*

*LESS THAN 0.5%.

Q.10B

TABLE 12

IMPORTANCE OF VICTIM/WITNESS ASSISTANCE PROGRAMS

Q.: How important do you think it is to have agencies that make (READ EACH ITEM) available to crime victims -- very important, somewhat important, not too important, or not important at all?

BASE: 448	VERY IMPORTANT %	SOMEWHAT IMPORTANT %	NOT TOO IMPORTANT %	NOT IMPORTANT AT ALL %	NOT SURE %
COMPENSATION FOR MEDICAL EXPENSES	80	14	2	2	2
LEGAL ASSISTANCE	78	16	1	2	2
INFORMATION ON YOUR CASE STATUS	74	17	3	3	2
COMPENSATION FOR LOSS OF EARNINGS OR SUPPORT	73	19	3	2	3
ASSISTANCE IN DEALING WITH THE POLICE, COURTS, OR SOCIAL SERVICES	70	21	3	4	2
SECURITY INFORMATION OR ASSISTANCE	68	21	5	3	3
EMOTIONAL OR PSYCHOLOGICAL COUNSELING	66	22	3	4	5
PERSONAL PROTECTION	66	21	5	3	5
THE PROPERTY BACK OR MONEY TO REPLACE THE PROPERTY	63	24	5	5	4
COMPENSATION FOR STOLEN PROPERTY	63	25	4	4	4
INFORMATION AND REFERRALS FOR SERVICES	62	28	4	3	3
DAY CARE FOR YOUR CHILDREN	56	26	6	6	6
TRANSPORTATION TO THE COURTS	51	30	10	6	3
RELOCATION OR HELP IN FINDING A NEW RESIDENCE	50	29	10	6	5

CHAPTER V: THE CRIME VICTIMS COMPENSATION BOARD

The Crime Victims Compensation Board is a specialized VWAP agency of the State of New York.   It makes awards to victims or their dependents who suffer serious financial hardship as a result of injuries sustained in violent crimes.   These awards may be made for unreimbursed medical expenses, losses of earnings or support, or funeral expenses.   Thus, the Board does not cover all types of VWAP services or all types of victims.   Even in this sample of victims of reported index crimes, only the 19% of victims who were injured as a result of the crime would be eligible claimants, and it is likely that the number of victims eligible for Board awards would be still smaller (e.g., only 15% received medical treatment).   Nevertheless, the knowledge and attitudes of victims regarding the Crime Victims Compensation Board are instructive, and we examine them in this chapter.

Awareness and Contacts

Only a little over one-third (35%) of the victims of index crimes in New York State who reported these crimes to the police were aware of the existence of the Crime Victims Compensation Board (Table 13).   A slightly larger proportion of those who suffered physical injuries than of those who were not injured knew of the Board (43% vs. 33%), but the difference is not statistically significant.   Awareness of the Board was lower among minority victims (28%) than among white victims (38%), and it was lower among those with annual family incomes below $15,000 (31%) than among those with higher incomes (42%).

The mass media were the primary means by which victims learned of the Crime Victims Compensation Board (Table 14). Newspapers (37%) and spot announcements on television and radio (31%) are cited far more often than other sources by those aware of the Board as the means by which they learned about it. In particular, only 3% of those who were aware of the Board say they heard about it from the police when they reported the crime; this represents only 1% of victims of index crimes who reported the crimes to the police. The proportion of victims told about the Board by the police is the same even among those who were injured as a result of the crime.

Observation:

The fact that so few victims heard of the Board from the police when reporting the crime is significant. By law, the police are required to inform injured victims of their potential eligibility for the Board's services. They are the primary means of direct contact with crime victims, and that contact occurs at the time when the information is salient to the victim. The mass media cannot substitute efficiently for the police. A top priority should be to increase the regularity with which the police inform victims about the Board, and about other VWAP programs.

Only 7% of those who knew about the Board filed a claim; this represents only 2% of victims of reported index crimes (Table 15). The proportions are somewhat higher among victims who sustained injuries; 23% of injured victims who were aware of the Board (or 10% of victims of reported index crimes who were injured as a result of the crime) filed claims.

The primary reason for not filing a claim was the expectation that not much would come of it. Among those who knew of the Board but didn't file a claim, 38% felt the claim would be too small to bother with, and 30% expected they would not qualify (Table 16). But some of the other reasons cited by those who did not file indicate a lack of awareness of the Board's services at that time: 15% did not know of the Board at the time; 10% never thought of going; and 9% were not aware of how to go about filing. To these should be added the 65% of all victims who were not aware of the Board, including 57% of victims who suffered injuries.

Observation:

Clearly there is room for increased awareness of the Crime Victims Compensation Board among victims. Even among injured victims of reported index crimes, only 1 in 10 file for claims. Some of those who do not may be ineligible for benefits, but some others are not receiving benefits for which they are eligible. Again, the critical role that can be played by the police is emphasized by the survey.

Q.12A

TABLE 13

AWARENESS OF CRIME VICTIMS COMPENSATION BOARD

Q.: Have you ever heard of the Crime Victims Compensation Board, or haven't you?

	BASE		YES, HAVE HEARD OF	NO, HAVEN'T HEARD OF	NOT SURE
TOTAL	447	%	35	64	1
COUNTY TYPE					
URBAN	334	%	37	62	1
SUBURBAN	85	%	31	69	-
RURAL	28	%	25	75	-
REGION					
METRO NEW YORK	294	%	37	63	*
UPSTATE	153	%	31	68	1
RACE					
WHITE	307	%	38	61	1
BLACK	91	%	31	68	1
HISPANIC	37	%	22	78	-
INCOME					
$15,000 OR LESS	188	%	31	68	1
$15,001-$35,000	161	%	42	57	1
$35,001 AND OVER	46	%	40	60	-
AGE					
UNDER 30 YEARS	136	%	18	81	1
30-64 YEARS	269	%	43	57	*
65 AND OVER	41	%	41	56	3

*LESS THAN 0.5%.

Q.12B

TABLE 14

HOW LEARNED OF CRIME VICTIMS COMPENSATION BOARD
BASE: HEARD OF CRIME VICTIMS COMPENSATION BOARD

Q.: How did you learn about the Crime Victims Compensation Board?

BASE	TOTAL 155 %
NEWSPAPERS	37
FROM SPOT ANNOUNCEMENTS ON RADIO AND TELEVISION	31
FRIENDS, RELATIVES, COWORKERS	12
FROM THE POLICE WHEN YOU REPORTED THE CRIME	3
FROM POSTERS IN THE MASS TRANSIT	2
FROM POSTERS IN HOSPITALS	1
FROM THE LIBRARY	1
FROM DISTRICT ATTORNEY'S OFFICE	-
FROM VICTIM WITNESS ASSISTANCE PROGRAMS	-
OTHER	19
NOT SURE	6

Q.13A

TABLE 15

FILED CLAIM WITH CRIME VICTIMS COMPENSATION BOARD
BASE: HEARD OF CRIME VICTIMS COMPENSATION BOARD

Q.: Did you, your dependent, legal guardian, or attorney file a claim with the Crime Victims Compensation Board, or not?

	TOTAL
BASE	153
	%
YES, DID FILE	7
NO, DIDN'T FILE	91
NOT SURE	3

Q.13B

TABLE 16

REASONS FOR NOT FILING A CLAIM WITH
CRIME VICTIMS COMPENSATION BOARD
BASE: HEARD OF CRIME VICTIMS COMPENSATION BOARD
AND DIDN'T FILE CLAIM

Q.: Why didn't you file a claim with the Crime Victims Compensation Board?
What other reasons?

	TOTAL
BASE	139
	%
CLAIM FOR LOSSES WAS TOO SMALL (E.G., RECOVERED FROM OTHER SOURCES, INCIDENT WAS TOO MINOR)	38
DIDN'T THINK I WOULD QUALIFY	30
DID NOT KNOW ABOUT CVCB AT THE TIME	15
TOO MUCH TROUBLE/BOTHER, NOT CONVENIENT	12
NOT INJURED	11
NEVER THOUGHT OF GOING	10
NOT AWARE OF HOW TO GET BENEFITS OR ELIGIBILITY	9
ALL OTHERS	11
NOT SURE	-

Attitudes of Victims toward the Crime Victims Compensation Board
==

Support for the Board is very strong among victims of reported index

crimes in New York State when its function is explained to them. More than 9

out of 10 victims (93%) approve of the service provided by the Board, and this

approval is high in all groups (Table 17).

Moreover, more than 7 out of 10 (71%) favor "providing more money to

be spent by the Crime Victims Compensation Board even if this meant a slight

increase in state taxes" (Table 18). Again, overwhelming support is

registered among every group in the sample.

The survey also provides data on victims' attitudes toward nine

specific proposals for changes in the state's policies on victim compensation

(Table 19). Victims support each of the proposed changes "even if the change

would cost more money for the state." The two most popular proposals shift

part of the burden of victim compensation to the convicted criminals.

> -- By 95-3%, victims favor "making convicted criminals pay
> back victims for property stolen, damaged, or lost
> during the crime";

> -- By 94-4%, victims favor "making convicted criminals help
> pay part of the cost of compensation and services for
> victims."

Two proposals that expand compensation to witnesses and "good

Samaritans" are the next most popular among victims.

> -- By 90-8%, they favor "paying more generous benefits to
> good Samaritans who are injured or killed trying to aid
> a crime victim";

> -- By 85-13%, they favor "compensating witnesses for their
> loss of earnings and travel expenses when testifying at
> a trial."

The less popular proposals all involve increasing the levels of

benefits to victims or expanding the definition of who is eligible for benefits. But although these garner less support than the others, majorities of victims favor each one.

Observation:

Victims of reported index crimes in the State of New York are strongly supportive of the Crime Victims Compensation Board. Although very few have benefited directly from the Board, victims support its existence and favor its expansion even if this were to mean a slight increase in the taxes they pay.

Q.18A

TABLE 17

APPROVAL OF CRIME VICTIMS COMPENSATION BOARD

Q.: The New York State Crime Victims Compensation Board may reimburse the innocent victim or dependent of an innocent victim who was injured, disabled, or killed as a result of a violent crime for unreimbursed medical expenses, earnings, funeral expenses, or loss of support.
Do you approve of New York State providing this service for victims of violent crimes, or not?

	BASE		YES, APPROVE	NO, DON'T APPROVE	NOT SURE
TOTAL	448	%	93	4	3
COUNTY TYPE					
URBAN	335	%	93	3	4
SUBURBAN	85	%	93	6	1
RURAL	28	%	82	14	4
REGION					
METRO NEW YORK	294	%	94	3	3
UPSTATE	154	%	89	7	4
RACE					
WHITE	308	%	92	6	3
BLACK	91	%	98	2	-
HISPANIC	37	%	86	-	14
INCOME					
$15,000 OR LESS	188	%	96	3	2
$15,001-$35,000	162	%	91	6	3
$35,001 AND OVER	46	%	96	4	-
AGE					
UNDER 30 YEARS	136	%	95	3	2
30-64 YEARS	270	%	91	6	3
65 AND OVER	41	%	93	-	7

Q.19

TABLE 18

SUPPORT FOR INCREASED EXPENDITURES BY
CRIME VICTIMS COMPENSATION BOARD

Q.: In general, would you favor the State of New York providing more money to be spent by the Crime Victims Compensation Board even if this meant a slight increase in state taxes, or would you oppose more money for the Crime Victims Compensation Board?

	BASE		FAVOR	OPPOSE	NOT SURE
TOTAL	448	%	71	19	10
COUNTY TYPE					
URBAN	335	%	73	17	10
SUBURBAN	85	%	66	23	11
RURAL	28	%	71	25	4
REGION					
METRO NEW YORK	294	%	72	17	10
UPSTATE	154	%	68	22	10
RACE					
WHITE	308	%	70	18	12
BLACK	91	%	72	25	2
HISPANIC	37	%	73	11	16
INCOME					
$15,000 OR LESS	188	%	71	21	8
$15,001-$35,000	162	%	73	16	11
$35,001 AND OVER	46	%	72	20	8
AGE					
UNDER 30 YEARS	136	%	66	24	10
30-64 YEARS	270	%	73	18	9
65 AND OVER	41	%	73	5	22

Q.20

TABLE 19

SUPPORT FOR PROPOSED CHANGES IN SERVICES TO CRIME VICTIMS

Q.: I would like to read you some changes being considered in New York State for providing services to crime victims. For each, please tell me whether you favor or oppose the change, even if the change would cost more money for the state.

BASE: 443

	FAVOR %	OPPOSE %	NOT SURE %
DO YOU FAVOR OR OPPOSE MAKING CONVICTED CRIMINALS PAY BACK VICTIMS FOR PROPERTY STOLEN, DAMAGED, OR LOST DURING THE CRIME?	95	3	2
DO YOU FAVOR OR OPPOSE MAKING CONVICTED CRIMINALS HELP PAY PART OF THE COST OF COMPENSATION AND SERVICES FOR VICTIMS?	94	4	2
DO YOU FAVOR OR OPPOSE PAYING MORE GENEROUS BENEFITS TO GOOD SAMARITANS WHO ARE INJURED OR KILLED TRYING TO AID A CRIME VICTIM?	90	8	3
DO YOU FAVOR OR OPPOSE COMPENSATING WITNESSES FOR THEIR LOSS OF EARNINGS AND TRAVEL EXPENSES WHEN TESTIFYING AT A TRIAL?	85	13	2
BURIAL EXPENSES CAN NOW ONLY BE REIMBURSED IF THEY ARE PAID BY A VICTIM'S SPOUSE, PARENTS, OR CHILDREN; DO YOU FAVOR OR OPPOSE REIMBURSING ANYONE WHO PAYS FOR A CRIME VICTIM'S BURIAL?	74	21	5
A PERSON WHO IS THE VICTIM OF A CRIME COMMITTED BY A MEMBER OF HIS OR HER FAMILY CANNOT NOW RECEIVE BENEFITS; DO YOU FAVOR OR OPPOSE ELIMINATING THIS CONDITION AND ALLOWING VICTIMS TO RECEIVE BENEFITS EVEN IF THE CRIME WAS COMMITTED BY A MEMBER OF THEIR FAMILY, PROVIDED THE OFFENDER WOULD NOT BENEFIT IN ANY WAY?	65	29	7
AT PRESENT, CRIME VICTIMS CAN ONLY RECEIVE MONEY FROM THE CRIME VICTIMS COMPENSATION BOARD IF THE CRIME RESULTS IN SERIOUS FINANCIAL HARDSHIP; DO YOU FAVOR OR OPPOSE ELIMINATING THIS CONDITION AND MAKING ALL CRIME VICTIMS ELIGIBLE TO RECEIVE COMPENSATION?	60	37	3
NEW YORK STATE NOW ONLY PROVIDES BENEFITS TO VICTIMS OF VIOLENT CRIMES; DO YOU FAVOR OR OPPOSE ELIMINATING THIS CONDITION SO THAT BENEFITS COULD BE PAID TO VICTIMS OF ANY CRIME?	57	38	5
THE MOST A CRIME VICTIM OR A VICTIM'S FAMILY CAN NOW RECEIVE FOR LOSS OF EARNINGS OR SUPPORT IS $20,000; DO YOU FAVOR OR OPPOSE INCREASING THIS LIMIT TO $50,000?	56	37	7

APPENDIX:

THE QUESTIONNAIRE

LOUIS HARRIS AND ASSOCIATES, INC.
630 Fifth Avenue, New York, N.Y. 10111

Study No. 802516-V

December 1980

FOR OFFICE USE ONLY:

Questionnaire No._____
                    5-6-7-8-9
Sample Point No. _____
                    10-11-12-13-14

Interviewer:(PLEASE PRINT)_____

City/Town_____ State:_____ Zip:_____

Hello, I'm_____from the Harris Poll. May I speak to (designated respondent)? We are conducting a survey for the State of New York about the criminal justice system and the needs of crime victims. We have already spoken to a number of crime victims about their experiences, and we would appreciate your help in answering some questons.

(IF ASKED): We got the names and telephone numbers of people who were crime victims in the last year from police departments in New York State.

We are talking to 500 crime victims because we feel that they are the ones best qualified to give their opinions about how the criminal justice system operates for the victims of crimes, and to help determine what can be done to help out the innocent victims of violent crime.

DESIGNATED RESPONDENT: _____

TELEPHONE NUMBER: _____

WHEN CRIME REPORTED: _____

FOR OFFICE USE ONLY:

Questionnaire No. _____
5-6-7-8-9

Sample Point No. _____
10-11-12-13-14

-1-   CARD 1   802516-V

1a. Police department records show that you reported that either you or a member of your family were the victim of a crime in the past twelve months. How would you describe that crime you reported -- was it a mugging, a robbery, an assault, a burglary, a rape, a murder, or what? (IF VICTIM MORE THAN ONCE: ASK ABOUT MOST RECENT TIME)

```
INTERVIEWER:   IF CRIME WAS MURDER OF FAMILY MEMBER, STOP AND USE MURDER VICTIM
QUESTIONNAIRE
```

/MULTIPLE RECORD/

Mugging..................(20(____ -1
Robbery.....................____ -2
Assault.....................____ -3
Burglary....................____ -4
Rape........................____ -5
Larceny.....................____ -6
Other (SPECIFY)

_____.....____ -7
Not sure/refused............____ -8

1b. Were you the victim of this crime or was someone else the victim?

Respondent victim..........(21(____ -1 ⎫ (CONTINUE WITH QUESTIONNAIRE)
Respondent and other..........____ -2 ⎭

Other victim...................____ -3   (IF "OTHER VICTIM" IS ADULT,
                                            AT LEAST 16 YEARS OLD, ASK TO
                                            SPEAK TO THAT PERSON;
                                            CONTINUE INTERVIEW WITH THAT
                                            PERSON.)

/ASK Q.1c ONLY FOR BURGLARY -- SKIP OTHERS TO Q.1d./
1c. Were you present when the crime was committed, or not?

Yes, present.(22(____ -1 (ASK Q.1d)

No, not present..____ -2 ⎫ (SKIP TO Q.2)
Not sure.........____ -3 ⎭

/ASK EVERYONE, EXCEPT "NOT PRESENT" OR "NOT SURE" IN Q.1c/
1d. Did the person who committed the crime have a weapon or not?

Yes, had weapon..........(23(____ -1 (SKIP TO Q.2)

No, didn't have..............____ -2 ⎫ (ASK Q.1e)
Not sure.....................____ -3 ⎭

1e. Were you threatened with the use of force or not?

Yes, threatened..............(24(____ -1
No, but I felt threatened (vol.).____ -2
No, not threatened...............____ -3
Not sure.........................____ -4

2. Did this crime occur in your home, near your home but in your neighborhood, where you work, near where you work, or where?

```
In your home................(25(____-1
Near home (including lobby,
   hallway, etc., of apartment
   building)......................____-2
At work.........................____-3
Near work.......................____-4
Elswhere (SPECIFY)

_____

_____

_____.....____-5
Not sure/refused...............____-6
```

3. What time of day did the crime occur?

```
A.M. hour..........___:___  (26-29)
P.M. hour..........___:___  (30-33)
Not sure/refused..........(34(____-1
```

4. How soon after the crime occurred did you report it to police?

```
0-10 mins.............(35(____-1
11-30 mins................____-2
31-60 mins................____-3
61 mins-2 hrs.............____-4
Over 2 hrs-4 hrs..........____-5
More than 4 hrs. (SPECIFY)

_____...____-6
Not sure/refused..........____-7
```

5. I'd like to know how you felt about the way the police handled your case. Overall, were you very satisfied, somewhat satisfied, somewhat dissatisfied, or very dissatisfied with the way the police handled your case?

```
Very satisfied............(36(____-1
Somewhat satisfied............____-2
Somewhat dissatisfied.........____-3
Very dissatisfied.............____-4
Not sure......................____-5
```

6. Was anyone ever arrested for this crime, or not?

> Yes, someone arrested.(37(___-1 (ASK Q.7a)
>
> No, no one arrested.......___-2 ⎫
> Not sure.................___-3 ⎭ (SKIP TO Q.8)

7a. How did you feel about the way the district attorney's office handled your case -- overall, were you very satisfed, somewhat satisfied, somewhat dissatisfied, or very dissatisfied with the way the district attorney's office handled your case?

> Very satisfied.............(38(___-1
> Somewhat satisfied..............___-2
> Somewhat dissatisfied...........___-3
> Very dissatisfied...............___-4
> Not sure.......................___-5

7b. Did the case go to trial, or not?

> Yes, went to trial...(39(___-1 (ASK Q.7c)
>
> No, did not go to trial..___-2 ⎫
> Not sure................___-3 ⎭ (SKIP TO Q.8)

7c. Was the suspect found guilty or not?

> Found guilty.........(40(___-1
> Not found guilty..........___-2
> Not sure..................___-3

7d. Did you appear as a witness at the trial, or not?

> Yes, appeared........(41(___-1
> No, didn't appear.........___-2
> Not sure..................___-3

7e. How satisfied were you with the outcome of the trial -- very satisfied, somewhat satisfied, somewhat dissatisfied, or very dissatisfied ?

> Very satisfied...........(42(___-1
> Somewhat satisfied...........___-2
> Somewhat dissatisfied........___-3
> Very dissatisfied...........___-4
> Not sure....................___-5

8. Now I'd like to read a series of statements about being the victim of a crime. Some crime victims agree with these statements; other crime victims disagree with these statements. On the basis of your experience, please tell me whether you agree strongly, agree somewhat, disagree somewhat, or disagree strongly with each statement?

/READ EACH ITEM/

/START AT "X"/

	Agree Strongly	Agree Somewhat	Disagree Somewhat	Disagree Strongly	No Experience/ Does Not Apply (Vol.)	Not Sure
( ) 1. The police responded quickly after they were told of the crime............(43(	-1	-2	-3	-4	-5	-6
( ) 2. The police treated me well..............(44(	-1	-2	-3	-4	-5	-6
( ) 3. The police did all they could to try to locate the criminal...(45(	-1	-2	-3	-4	-5	-6
( ) 4. I was not kept informed about what was happening during the police investigation of the crime.....(46(	-1	-2	-3	-4	-5	-6
( ) 5. I was not kept informed of what was happening during the trial......(47(	-1	-2	-3	-4	-5	-6
( ) 6. Identifying a subject or testifying in court is dangerous because they may try to get even with you..(48(	-1	-2	-3	-4	-5	-6
( ) 7. After my experience in this case, I wouldn't ever bother to get involved with the police or the courts again......(49(	-1	-2	-3	-4	-5	-6
( ) 8. Nobody in the criminal justice system seems to care about the victim......(50(	-1	-2	-3	-4	-5	-6
( ) 9. During the whole period I was treated more like the criminal than like the victim..(51(	-1	-2	-3	-4	-5	-6
( ) 10. The whole experience of the investigation and trial was very disturbing to me.(52(	-1	-2	-3	-4	-5	-6
( ) 11. I will never take the chance of testifying against someone because the punishment they would get is not worth the risk they will try to get even.......(53(	-1	-2	-3	-4	-5	-6
( ) 12. Being the victim of a crime changed my whole life and made me more fearful about becoming a victim............(54(	-1	-2	-3	-4	-5	-6
( ) 13. Since the crime, I am much more careful about what I do and where I go.......(55(	-1	-2	-3	-4	-5	-6

9a. I'm going to read you a list of things that might have happened to you as a result of being a crime victim. Please tell me which ones actually happened to you. To start with, did you (READ EACH ITEM) or not?

/GO THROUGH FULL LIST FOR Q.9a; THEN ASK Q.9b AND Q.9c CONSECUTIVELY FOR EACH "YES" IN Q.9a./

/START AT "X"/

	Q.9a			Q.9b		Q.9c	
	Yes	No	Not Sure	Dollar Value	Not Sure	Percent Recovered	Not Sure
( ) 1. Lose time from work because of injuries....	(56( )-1	_-2	_-3	$____ (70-74)	(75( )-1	____% (76-78)	(79( )-1
( ) 2. Lose time from work to provide information to police for the investigation....	(57( )-1	_-2	_-3	$____ (10-14)	(15( )-1	____% (16-18)	(19( )-1
( ) 3. Lose time from work to assist the district attorney or take part in the trial....	(58( )-1	_-2	_-3	$____ (20-24)	(25( )-1	____% (26-28)	(29( )-1
( ) 4. Have money or property stolen....	(59( )-1	_-2	_-3	$____ (30-34)	(35( )-1	____% (36-38)	(39( )-1
( ) 5. Have property damaged or destroyed....	(60( )-1	_-2	_-3	$____ (40-44)	(45( )-1	____% (46-48)	(49( )-1
( ) 6. Personally receive any physical injuries as a result of the crime....	(61( )-1	_-2	_-3	XXXXXXXXXXXXXXXXXXXXXXXXXXXXXXXXXXXXXXXXXXX			
( ) 7. Receive medical treatment or spend time in the hospital as a result of injuries....	(62( )-1	_-2	_-3	$____ (50-54)	(55( )-1	____% (56-58)	(59( )-1

/63-69/

/ASK FOR EACH "YES" IN Q.9a/
9b. I would like you to estimate the dollar value of each of these things. For instance, how much would you estimate it cost you in dollars to (READ EACH ITEM "YES" IN Q.9a)?

/ASK FOR EACH DOLLAR VALUE GREATER THAN ZERO IN Q.9b/
9c. What percentage of this cost would you estimate you recovered through insurance or any other means?

10a. After the crime occurred, did you receive (READ EACH ITEM) from any social service or government agency? /RECORD BELOW/

/START AT "X"/	Q.10a Yes	No	Does Not Apply (Vol.)	Not Sure	Q.10b Very Important	Somewhat Important	Not Too Important	Not Important At All	Not Sure
( ) 1. Emotional or psychological counseling........(60(	-1	-2	-3	-4	(10(-1	-2	-3	-4	-5
( ) 2. The property back or money to replace the property.........(61(	-1	-2	-3	-4	(11(-1	-2	-3	-4	-5
( ) 3. Transportation to the courts......(62(	-1	-2	-3	-4	(12(-1	-2	-3	-4	-5
( ) 4. Information on your case status...(63(	-1	-2	-3	-4	(13(-1	-2	-3	-4	-5
( ) 5. Day care for your children......(64(	-1	-2	-3	-4	(14(-1	-2	-3	-4	-5
( ) 6. Compensation for medical expenses..........(65(	-1	-2	-3	-4	(15(-1	-2	-3	-4	-5
( ) 7. Compensation for loss of earnings or support....(66(	-1	-2	-3	-4	(16(-1	-2	-3	-4	-5
( ) 8. Compensation for stolen property..........(67(	-1	-2	-3	-4	(17(-1	-2	-3	-4	-5
( ) 9. Personal protection.........(68(	-1	-2	-3	-4	(18(-1	-2	-3	-4	-5
( ) 10. Legal assistance.........(69(	-1	-2	-3	-4	(19(-1	-2	-3	-4	-5
( ) 11. Security information or assistance.........(70(	-1	-2	-3	-4	(20(-1	-2	-3	-4	-5
( ) 12. Relocation or help in finding a new residence......(71(	-1	-2	-3	-4	(21(-1	-2	-3	-4	-5
( ) 13. Information and referrals for services..........(72(	-1	-2	-3	-4	(22(-1	-2	-3	-4	-5
( ) 14. Assistance in dealing with the police, courts, or social services....(73(	-1	-2	-3	-4	(23(-1	-2	-3	-4	-5

10b. How important do you think it is to have agencies that make (READ EACH ITEM) available to crime victims -- very important, somewhat important, not too important, or not important at all? /RECORD ABOVE/

11. As a result of the incident, (was/were) (READ EACH ITEM) a very serious problem, somewhat serious, not too serious, or not a problem at all?

/START AT "X"/	Very Serious	Somewhat Serious	Not Too Serious	Not A Problem At All	Not Sure
( ) 1. Mental or emotional suffering......(24(	___-1	___-2	___-3	___-4	__-5
( ) 2. Physical injury....................(25(	___-1	___-2	___-3	___-4	__-5
( ) 3. Property loss......................(26(	___-1	___-2	___-3	___-4	__-5
( ) 4. Time lost from your work..........(27(	___-1	___-2	___-3	___-4	__-5
( ) 5. Income loss.......................(28(	___-1	___-2	___-3	___-4	__-5
( ) 6. Insurance problems................(29(	___-1	___-2	___-3	___-4	__-5
( ) 7. Problems with your family.........(30(	___-1	___-2	___-3	___-4	__-5
( ) 8. Problems with your job............(31(	___-1	___-2	___-3	___-4	__-5

12a. Have you ever heard of the Crime Victims Compensation Board, or haven't you?

Yes, have heard of.........(32(_____-1 (ASK Q.12b)

No, haven't heard of..........._____-2 ⎞
Not sure......................_____-3 ⎠ (SKIP TO Q.18a)

12b. How did you learn about the Crime Victims Compensation Board?

/DO NOT READ CATEGORIES. MULTIPLE RECORD BELOW/

From the police when you reported the crime...........(33(_____-1
From posters in hospitals......................................_____-2
From District Attorney's Office................................_____-3
From the library..._____-4
From posters in the mass transit..............................._____-5
From spot announcements on radio and television..........._____-6
From Victim Witness Assistance Programs..................._____-7
Other (SPECIFY)

_____..._____-8
Not sure..._____-9

13a. Did you, your dependent, legal guardian, or attorney file a claim with the Crime Victims Compensation Board, or not?

        Yes, did file.............(34(_____-1 (SKIP TO Q.14)

        No, didn't file................_____-2 (ASK Q.13b)

        Not sure......................._____-3 (SKIP TO Q.18a)

13b. Why didn't you file a claim with the Crime Victims Compensation Board? What other reasons?

_____(35(_____

_____(36(_____   } (SKIP TO Q.18a)

_____(37(_____

14. Were you contacted by an investigator from the Crime Victims Compensation Board, or not?

        Yes, was contacted..........(38(_____-1
        No, was not contacted..........._____-2
        Not sure........................._____-3

15. Did you receive any benefits from the Crime Victims Compensation Board, or not?

        Yes, did receive........(39(___-1 (SKIP TO Q.17)

        No, didn't receive..........___-2 (ASK Q.16)

        Case not resolved yet (vol.)___-3 ⎫
        Not sure....................___-4 ⎭ (SKIP TO Q.17)

16. Were you told why your claim was not accepted, or weren't you?

Yes, was told........(40(____-1
No, wasn't told..........____-2
Not sure.................____-3

17. Overall, how would you rate the job being done by the Crime Victims Compensation Board -- excellent, pretty good, only fair, or poor?

Excellent.........(41(____-1
Pretty good...........____-2
Only fair.............____-3
Poor..................____-4
Not sure.............____-5

/ASK EVERYONE/

18a. The New York State Crime Victims Compensation Board may reimburse the innocent victim or dependent of an innocent victim who was injured, disabled, or killed as a result of a violent crime for unreimbursed medical expenses, earnings, funeral expenses, or loss of support.
Do you approve of New York State providing this service for victims of violent crimes, or not?

Yes, approve..........(42(____-1 ⎫ (ASK Q.18b)
No, don't approve.........____-2 ⎭

Not sure.................____-3 (SKIP TO Q.19)

18b. How strongly do you (approve/disapprove) of New York State providing this service -- strongly or weakly?

Strongly.......(43(____-1
Weakly.............____-2
Not sure...........____-3

/ASK EVERYONE/

19. In general, would you favor the State of New York providing more money to be spent by the Crime Victims Compensation Board even if this meant a slight increase in state taxes, or would you oppose more money for the Crime Victims Compensation Board?

Favor.............(44(____-1
Oppose...............____-2
Not sure.............____-3

20. I would like to read you some changes being considered in New York State for providing services to crime victims. For each, please tell me whether you favor or oppose the change, even if the change would cost more money for the state.

/READ EACH ITEM/

/START AT "X"/   Favor Oppose Not Sure

( ) 1. At present, crime victims can only receive money from the Crime Victims Compensation Board if the crime results in serious financial hardship; do you favor or oppose eliminating this condition and making all crime victims eligible to receive compensation?.........................(45(___-1 ___-2 ___-3

( ) 2. Do you favor or oppose making convicted criminals help pay part of the cost of compensation and services for victims?...(46(___-1 ___-2 ___-3

( ) 3. The most a crime victim or a victim's family can now receive for loss of earnings or support is $20,000; do you favor or oppose increasing this limit to $50,000?.....(47(___-1 ___-2 ___-3

( ) 4. A person who is the victim of a crime committed by a member of his or her family cannot now receive benefits; do you favor or oppose eliminating this condition and allowing victims to receive benefits even if the crime was committed by a member of their family, provided the offender would not benefit in any way?....................(48(___-1 ___-2 ___-3

( ) 5. Burial expenses can now only be reimbursed if they are paid by a victim's spouse, parents, or children; do you favor or oppose reimbursing anyone who pays for a crime victim's burial?.................................(49(___-1 ___-2 ___-3

( ) 6. Do you favor or oppose paying more generous benefits to Good Samaritans who are injured or killed trying to aid a crime victim?..(50(___-1 ___-2 ___-3

( ) 7. New York State now only provides benefits to victims of violent crimes; do you favor or oppose eliminating this condition so that benefits could be paid to victims of any crime?..(51(___-1 ___-2 ___-3

( ) 8. Do you favor or oppose compensating witnesses for their loss of earnings and travel expenses when testifying at a trial?..(52(___-1 ___-2 ___-3

( ) 9. Do you favor or oppose making convicted criminals pay back victims for property stolen, damaged, or lost during the crime?..(53(___-1 ___-2 ___-3

21a. Do you think that you would file a claim with the Crime Victims Compensation Board if you were a victim of a violent crime in the future?

> Yes, would.........(54(_____-1 (SKIP TO Q.22a)
>
> No, wouldn't..........._____-2 (ASK Q.21b)
>
> Not sure..............._____-3 (SKIP TO Q.22a)

21b. Why not? What else?

_____ (55(

_____ (56(

_____ (57(

/ASK EVERYONE/

22a. Have you ever been the victim of any other crime, or haven't you?

> Yes, have...........(58(_____-1 (ASK Q.22b)
>
> No, haven't.............._____-2 ⎱
> Not sure..............._____-3 ⎰ (SKIP TO Q.F1)

22b. How many other times have you been the victim of a crime?

(WRITE IN NUMBER) _____ (59-60)
> Not sure/refused.......(61(_____-1

22c. When was the most recent <u>other</u> time you were a victim of a crime?

> Within six months..............(62(_____-1
> Six months to one year ago........._____-2
> Over one year to two years ago....._____-3
> Over two years ago................._____-4
> Not sure/refused..................._____-5

/TO BE ASKED OF EVERYONE/

F1. What type of work does the main wage earner of this household do?

DESCRIBE JOB BRIEFLY:

```
Professional.................................(63(_____ -1
Manager, official.................................._____ -2
Proprietor (small business)......................._____ -3
Clerical worker..................................._____ -4
Sales worker......................................_____ -5
Skilled craftsman, foreman........................_____ -6
Operative, unskilled laborer (except farm)....._____ -7
Service worker...................................._____ -8
Farmer, farm manager, farm laborer.............._____ -9
Student..........................................._____ -0
Housewife........................................._____ -x
Military service.................................._____ -y
Unemployed.................................(64(_____ -1
Retired..........................................._____ -2
Welfare..........................................._____ -3
Disabled.........................................._____ -4
Other (SPECIFY)

_____......._____ -5
Not sure/refused.............................._____ -6
```

F2. How old are you? /IF HESITANT, READ LIST/

```
              16 to 20.....(65(_____ -1
              21 to 24........._____ -2
              25 to 29........._____ -3
              30 to 34........._____ -4
              35 to 39........._____ -5
              40 to 49........._____ -6
              50 to 64........._____ -7
              65 and over......_____ -8
              Refused.........._____ -9
```

F3. What was the last grade of school you completed?

```
              No formal schooling..........(66(____ -1
              First through 7th grade..........____ -2
              8th grade........................____ -3
              Some high school.................____ -4
              High school graduate.............____ -5
              Some college.....................____ -6
              Two-year college graduate........____ -7
              Four-year college graduate.......____ -8
              Postgraduate.....................____ -9
              Trade/technical/vocational
                 after high school*...........XXXXXX
              Refused..........................____ -0
```

/*INTERVIEWER: ASK FOR DETAILS, AND CODE INTO ONE OF THE ABOVE CATEGORIES./

F4. Which of the the following income categories best describes your total 1979 household income? Was it (READ LIST)?

$7,500 or less.......(67(_____ -1
$7,501 to $15,000........ _____ -2
$15,001 to $25,000....... _____ -3
$25,001 to $35,000....... _____ -4
$35,001 to $50,000....... _____ -5
$50,001 or over.......... _____ -6
Not sure/no answer/
    refused................ _____ -7

F5. Do you consider yourself white, black, Spanish-American, or what?

White, but <u>not</u> Hispanic...................(68(_____ -1
Black, but <u>not</u> Hispanic...................... _____ -2
Spanish-American (Mexican, Cuban, Puerto
    Rican, Central or South American)......... _____ -3
Asian (Oriental) or Pacific Islander......... _____ -4
American Indian or Alaskan native............ _____ -5
Not sure..................................... _____ -6

Thank you very much for your cooperation!

F6. Sex: /BY OBSERVATION -- DO NOT ASK/

Male......(69(___ -1
Female........___ -2

D